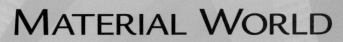

Rubber

by Claire Llewellyn

W
FRANKLIN WATTS
LONDON·SYDNEY

First published in 2001 by
Franklin Watts
96 Leonard Street
London EC2A 4XD

Franklin Watts Australia
56 O'Riordan Street
Alexandria
NSW 2015

Text copyright © Claire Llewellyn 2001

ISBN 0 7496 3989 X

Dewey Decimal
Classification Number: 678

A CIP catalogue record for this book is
available from the British Library

Series editor: Rosalind Beckman
Series designer: James Evans
Picture research: Sue Mennell
Photography: Steve Shott

Printed in Hong Kong, China

Acknowledgements

Thanks are due to the following for kind permission to
reproduce photographs:

Robert Harding Picture Library pp. 18b and back cover
(John Miller), 16-17
Corbis Images pp. 8t (Chinch Gryniewicz/ Ecoscene),
15t (Charles E. Rotkin), 23t (Charles E. Rotkin),
27b (James Marshall)
Garden Matters p. 16 (Colin Milkins)
Harry Cory-Wright p. 15b
NASA p. 25
Popperfoto pp. 10 (Dave Joiner/PPP), 11b (Dave Joiner/PPP)
Still Pictures pp. 17 (Ron Giling), 18t (Mark Edwards),
19 (Ron Giling), 21t (Mark Edwards), 23b (Mark Edwards)
Telegraph Colour Library pp. 8b (Barry Willis), 12b (Chris
Ladd), 14 (F.P.G./C.Benes), 26 (Curtis Martin), 27t (V.C.L.)
Tun Abdul Razak Research Centre pp. 20, 21b

Thanks are also due to the following for their help with this
book: Barnard Associates Optometrists; International Rubber
Study Group, London UK; John Lewis

Contents

Words printed in **bold italic** are explained in the glossary.

What is rubber?

Rubber is a very useful material. It is also a very safe material that can be used by everyone, even tiny babies.

Made of rubber

Rubber is used to make thousands of different things. These things are all around us – in houses, hospitals, factories, schools, swimming pools, offices and cars.

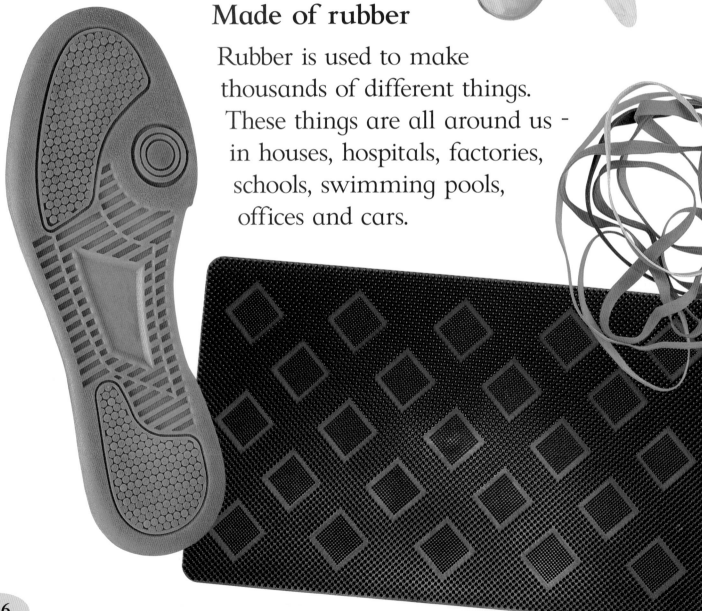

All the things in these pictures are made of rubber.
Can you name them all?

What do all these things feel like?
Do they all feel the same?

Material words
Which of these words describe rubber?

cold   thick   shiny

sticky   stretchy

heavy   stiff   solid

soft   strong

dull   hard   warm

hard-wearing

spongy   light

crisp

colourful

rough   smooth

thin

bendy   slimy

springy

runny

squashy

Fantastic fact

Rubber got its name because it can be used to rub out the marks made by a pencil.

Rubber is bendy and stretchy

Rubber is different from most other materials because it can bend and stretch. This makes it very special.

A fireman's hose needs to bend easily as it is pulled towards the fire.

The rubber hose on this paint sprayer allows it to reach every part of the car.

Things that bend

Some materials are hard and stiff, but rubber is soft and **flexible**. This means it can easily bend and curl. Firemen's hoses are made of rubber so that they will bend easily to reach the fire. Some electric tools have **flex** made of rubber because it is strong and can be pulled around buildings.

Things that stretch

When you pull rubber, it stretches. When you let it go, it springs back into shape. Swimming goggles have rubber straps. The strap stretches over your head, then springs back to give a good fit.

These goggles and swimming hat are made of rubber. They stretch to give a tight fit.

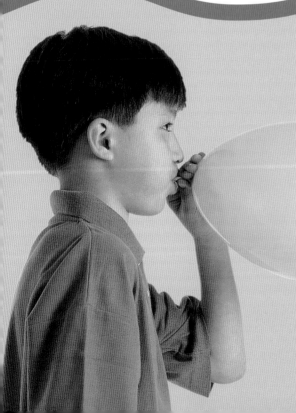

Try this

Blow up three balloons. Let the air out of the first one after ten seconds; out of the second one after an hour; and out of the third one after 24 hours. Do all the balloons spring back into shape?

Rubber is springy

Rubber is a springy material. It bounces off things that are hard. It takes the shock out of knocks and bumps, and helps to stop things breaking.

Bouncing about

If you drop a glass, it smashes on the ground. But if you drop a rubber ball, it will bounce back up again. Rubber's bounciness is a lot of fun. That's why rubber is used to make balls for tennis, basketball and other games.

Many sports such as tennis are played with balls that have rubber inside them.

Keeping you comfortable

Rubber is often used on the soles and heels of shoes. It makes shoes springy so that they soak up the shock when your feet hit the ground. This makes walking more comfortable and helps to protect the tiny bones in your feet.

Trainers keep you comfortable and protect your feet.

Bicycle tyres are tubes of rubber that are pumped full of air. The bouncy tyres roll over bumps in the road and give a more comfortable ride.

Bicycle tyres are made to be comfortable even on long, hard journeys.

Fantastic fact

The first bikes had wooden wheels that bumped along the road. They were so uncomfortable that they were called 'bone shakers'.

Rubber is waterproof

Rubber is a **waterproof** material. It does not let water or other **liquids** through. It also stops bottles from leaking.

Keeping dry

Rubber can be made into waterproof cloth. The cloth is perfect for babies' pants and for mattress protectors on cots and prams. Rubber is also used to make all sorts of wet-weather gear, such as coats, trousers and hats. A thin layer of rubber helps to waterproof other materials that often get wet, such as the cloth used for aprons and tablecloths.

Cleaning up spilled oil is dirty work. Rubber clothing keeps these workers clean and dry.

Stopping leaks

Rubber keeps water where you want it. Hot-water bottles are made of rubber to keep the water in. In the kitchen, rubber rings and stoppers give a tight seal to bottles and jars.

Keeping water out

Water and *electricity* must be kept apart. A waterproof rubber flex keeps water locked out, and dangerous electricity locked in.

rubber ring

Try this

Test whether rubber is waterproof. Fill a rubber glove with water. Does any of the water drip through?

13

Rubber is strong

Rubber is a very strong, hard-wearing material. It is sometimes used in machines and buildings that get a lot of use.

Preventing damage

Rubber is often used as a building material in bridges and **skyscrapers**. It helps to make them more stable. In places where there are **earthquakes**, rubber is often used in the **foundations** of buildings. It helps to absorb, or soak up, the shock of the earthquake and lessen the damage.

Los Angeles is in a part of the United States where earthquakes happen. Rubber is used in the foundations of the buildings to prevent them from collapsing.

Hard wearing

Rubber is used on **conveyor belts** and moving pavements because it is flexible and very strong.

Rubber conveyor belts are often used to move items from one part of a factory to another.

Rubber also makes a hard-wearing floor covering. It is often used in busy public places such as stations and airports. It is springy to walk on, gives a good grip for shoes and helps to cut down on noise.

Rubber tyres have to be tough because they carry a lot of weight.

Fantastic fact

The largest trucks have rubber tyres that are nearly 4 m (12 ft) high. Even a tall person reaches only halfway up a tyre.

Rubber comes from trees

Rubber is a **natural** material. It is made from **latex**, a milky white juice that is found inside plants.

The rubber tree

Latex is found in many plants. However, the latex in the rubber tree contains more rubber than any other plant. The scientific name of the rubber tree is *hevea*, but most people just call it the rubber tree.

Latex runs out of some plants if you cut them, as this picture shows.

Rubber *plantations*

Rubber trees are narrow, straight and tall. They grow in places near the *Equator*, in the warmest, wettest parts of the world. Most of the world's rubber comes from trees that are grown in huge plantations in the *Far East*.

The fully-grown trees of a rubber plantation.

Fantastic fact

Wild rubber trees were first found in South America. People took seeds from these trees and then planted them in other parts of the world. This is how plantations started.

This is a new rubber plantation and the trees are still very small. In time they will grow as tall as the trees in the picture above.

17

Collecting the latex

Latex is easy to collect. Plantation workers make a cut in the bark of a rubber tree and wait for the latex to drip out. This is known as 'tapping' the tree.

Plantation workers use a special curved knife to cut into the rubber tree.

Tapping the tree

The latex inside a rubber tree flows in tiny tubes inside the bark. To collect the latex, plantation workers make a thin, curving cut in the bark, then fix a spout and a cup at the bottom. Latex drips along the cut and into the cup. Rubber trees can be tapped when they are seven years old. They will produce latex for about 30 years.

The milky latex runs into the cup.

Collecting the latex

When the cups are full, they are emptied into buckets. Latex spoils easily after tapping so it must be made into solid rubber as soon as possible. This is usually done at the plantation.

Collecting the latex. A rubber tree is tapped every four days.

Fantastic fact

A rubber tree produces up to 4 gallons (15 l) of latex a year.

From latex to rubber

Solid rubber has to be separated from the latex. It is made into sheets or blocks, which are shipped all over the world.

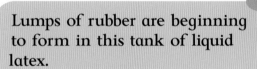

Lumps of rubber are beginning to form in this tank of liquid latex.

Removing the rubber

The latex is poured into long, narrow tanks, where it is strained to remove bits of dirt. *Acid* is then added to the tanks. The acid turns the rubber in the latex into solid lumps, which rise up and float on the surface.

Try this

Put two tablespoons of milk into a glass and stir in two tablespoons of vinegar. After a few seconds, you will see that the acid in the vinegar makes the milk turn lumpy. This is what happens when acid is added to latex.

Making rubber sheets

The rubber lumps are passed through rollers. The rollers squeeze out the water and press the lumps into rubbery sheets. The sheets are hung up in a warm place to dry for several days. Then they are made into **bales**, loaded on to ships, and sent to factories around the world.

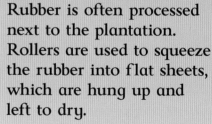

Rubber is often processed next to the plantation. Rollers are used to squeeze the rubber into flat sheets, which are hung up and left to dry.

Sometimes machines squash the rubber into blocks.

Making rubber goods

The bales of dry rubber arrive at the factory. Here the rubber is treated and shaped to make many different things.

Treating the rubber

Dry rubber is treated in different ways. It is mixed with other materials and heated to make it soft and easy to handle. It is also mixed with chemicals. Different chemicals can make rubber hard or strong, or as springy as a sponge.

The rubber *teat* of a baby's bottle is soft enough to suck and strong enough to chew.

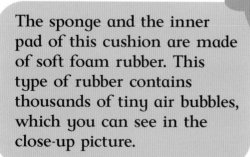

The sponge and the inner pad of this cushion are made of soft foam rubber. This type of rubber contains thousands of tiny air bubbles, which you can see in the close-up picture.

22

Shaping the rubber

Rubber can be made into many different shapes. It is rolled flat for flooring or doormats. It is squeezed through holes to make pipes and tubes. It is pushed into **moulds** to make things such as hot-water bottles and tyres.

These tyres have been shaped in a mould.

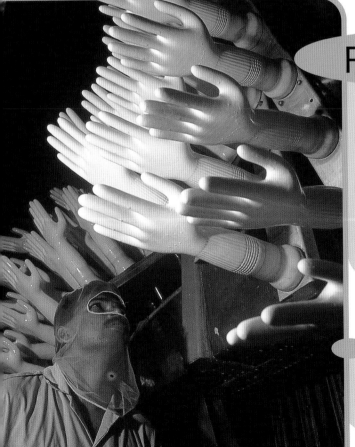

Fantastic fact

Thin, stretchy rubber objects such as balloons are made from latex instead of dry rubber. Moulds are dipped into the liquid latex before being left to dry.

Rubber gloves are made by dipping moulds into liquid rubber and leaving them to dry.

Rubber without trees

Not all rubber is made from latex.
Rubber can also be made from chemicals.
This material is known as
synthetic rubber.

kitchen spatula

Using chemicals

About 100 years ago, scientists began to
study natural rubber. They examined
its chemical make-up to see what
was in it. Over the years they
have learned to copy it by using
chemicals made from oil. These
chemicals form a material that
is like natural rubber, and can
often be used in its place. Many
of the items we use every day
are made of synthetic rubber.

baby teether

potato peeler

Synthetic rubber

Scientists are always searching for new materials. They have **experimented** with various chemicals to make new kinds of synthetic rubber. Some of these materials are stronger than natural rubber and can stand up to hotter temperatures. This means that synthetic rubber can be used in spacecraft, power stations and other places where natural rubber cannot.

Natural rubber is not strong enough to stand the heat and cold of space. A special type of synthetic rubber is used instead.

Fantastic fact

More than half of all the rubber we now use is synthetic. It is cheaper to make than natural rubber.

Recycling rubber

Most of the world's rubber is used to make tyres. Millions of them are made every year. Getting rid of old tyres is a serious problem. **Recycling** could be the answer.

Getting rid of tyres

It is not easy to get rid of old tyres because rubber does not rot. Burying or burning old tyres makes *gases* that *pollute* the air. Storing tyres is a fire risk, and could provide shelter for rats and other pests.

Part of a huge dump of unwanted tyres.

Recycling tyres

Old tyres can be cut up into tiny chips. These can be used to make floor coverings or a safe rubber surface for playgrounds or sports tracks. They can also be used in pavements, runways and roads. Rubber makes these surfaces quieter and helps them to last longer.

An old tyre makes the perfect swing.

This path of recycled rubber makes it easy to walk on the sand.

Fantastic fact

There are about 2 billion old tyres in the United States alone – and 250 million more are added every year.

Glossary

Acid A strong substance with a sharp or sour taste. Some acids are poisonous. Vinegar is a mild acid and is safe to use with food.

Bale A large bundle.

Conveyor belt A moving rubber belt used in places such as factories to move goods along.

Earthquake A sudden movement deep inside the Earth. Earthquakes make the ground shake, damaging buildings and bridges.

Electricity A useful sort of energy that can be used to make heat and light, and to power a motor.

Equator An imaginary line around the middle of the Earth, halfway between the North and South Poles.

Experiment To try out something new.

Far East A part of the world that contains many countries, including Thailand, Malaysia, Indonesia and China.

Flex The wire that comes from an electric machine and is coated with rubber or plastic.

Flexible Able to bend easily.

Foundation The solid stonework under a building. Foundations are built in holes in the ground to support the building above.

Gas A substance that is neither a liquid nor a solid, such as air.

Latex The thick, milky juice in some plants. The latex of the rubber tree contains a lot of rubber.

Liquid A runny substance such as water that has no shape.

Mould A container with a special shape. Rubber can be pushed into a mould to take on its shape.

Natural Found in the world around us.

Plantation A large piece of land that is used to grow one type of plant such as rubber trees.

Pollute To spoil or poison the air, land or water with harmful substances.

Recycle To take an object or material and use it to make something else.

Skyscraper A tall building with many floors.

Synthetic Not natural; made by people.

Teat The soft mouthpiece on a baby's bottle.

Waterproof Something that does not let water through.

Index